Samuel Wilberforce

The Revelation of God the Probation of Man

Two Sermons Preached Before the University of Oxford, on Sunday, Jan.

27, and Sunday, Feb. 3, 1861

Samuel Wilberforce

The Revelation of God the Probation of Man
*Two Sermons Preached Before the University of Oxford, on Sunday, Jan. 27, and
Sunday, Feb. 3, 1861*

ISBN/EAN: 9783337160029

Printed in Europe, USA, Canada, Australia, Japan

Cover: Foto ©Lupo / pixelio.de

More available books at **www.hansebooks.com**

The Revelation of God the Probation of Man.

TWO SERMONS

PREACHED BEFORE

THE UNIVERSITY OF OXFORD,

ON

SUNDAY, JAN. 27, AND SUNDAY, FEB. 3, 1861.

BY

SAMUEL, LORD BISHOP OF OXFORD,

LORD HIGH ALMONER TO HER MAJESTY THE QUEEN, AND
CHANCELLOR OF THE ORDER OF THE GARTER.

Oxford & London:

J. H. AND JAS. PARKER.

JOHN MURRAY, ALBEMARLE-STREET, LONDON.

1861.

MANY who heard these Sermons, and some of those for whose sake specially these subjects were selected, have so earnestly asked for their immediate publication, that I have felt it my duty to comply with their wish, although by doing so I leave necessarily much unsaid which I should have wished to add to guard myself from misconstruction. In particular, I should have wished to mark out the distinction between religious enquiry into the Revelation and sinful doubts concerning it. For Christianity has nothing to lose, and all to gain, from the fullest enquiry, if only it be humbly and faithfully conducted.

S. OXON.

SERMON I.

Neglect of the Revelation.

ST. JOHN xii. 37.

"BUT THOUGH HE HAD DONE SO MANY MIRACLES BEFORE THEM, YET
THEY BELIEVED NOT ON HIM."

WHAT an unspeakable sadness is there in the very
sound of these words! they breathe on us as the
sigh of an infinite compassion over a hopeless loss; they
sink into the heart with the heavy weight of a grief
which can know no remedy, no end. They speak of a
generation for whose salvation God had done in vain
all that He could do. Before their eyes Christ had
wrought His marvels; before them He had fulfilled the
voice of ancient prophecy; to them He had shewn His
countenance of love; in their ears He had spoken His
words of mercy: "but though He had done so many
miracles before them, yet they believed not on Him."
Surely in those words we may hear the tramp of the
avenging legions which ere long circled in the doomed
city, the yell of its intestine hatred, the faint sob of its
famine, the long wild cry of its despair; and rising high
above all these, the agony of each separate soul of all the
unbelieving multitude, as one by one they passed from
the rejection of salvation into the blackness of the outer
darkness.

These are the deep shadows, my brethren, which are
cast by the glowing lights of Epiphany. For Christ

B 2

manifested implies, alas! in impenitent hearts, Christ rejected. Evermore, as the generations of men in His Church pass in their day of trial before the eternal throne, the awful scene renews itself. "Though He had done so many miracles before them, yet they believed not on Him." God's revelation of Himself, the Redeemer's love, the Spirit's work; these, combined with the mystery of man's probation, imply acceptance and rejection; and these are but other words for salvation and despair, for life everlasting and eternal death.

To such thoughts, then, as these, Epiphany summons us. For in this scene of wonders *we* are now the actors; it is *our* eternal salvation which is staked upon the issue; we at this time are those who are being tried by the temptations which inseparably wait upon receiving a revelation from God; and as others, like ourselves, have failed under this trial, we ought in their failure to see our own danger, and so be led to examine carefully how far we are resisting its approaches.

It is to this most practical question that I desire, God helping me, to call your attention this afternoon. May He, without whose blessing the preacher's words are but empty sounds, speak by me to your inmost hearts.

Now there are many separate temptations to which the reception of a revelation from God must expose us, and these will assail different men with very different power. But there is one by which all must be tried, and it is to that one that I would confine myself to-day: I mean the temptation to neglect it; and in examining this danger there are four points to which I would specially call your attention.

I. To the different modes in which the presence of the evil is manifested.

II. To the causes which expose us to the evil.

III. To the consequences of yielding to it.

IV. To the escape from it.

I. And first, for the different manifestations of the evil. Now in entering on this subject, we must first have a clear idea of *what* the evil is. It is in its essential character entirely distinct from disbelief; there is about its victim no consciousness of rejecting revelation; nor, in many cases, even of doubting about it. It is not that its difficulties trouble his thoughts, or that its evidences are insufficient to convince him; it is that he does not think, or at least think really and deeply, about it. Most probably, amongst ourselves, he readily admits its truth; has no doubt about it; has never taken the trouble even to doubt; the tacit admission of its truth is like the acting of some involuntary law of his bodily life, an unconscious process of his existence. But it produces no effect upon him; it passes wholly by him; it is to him as if it was not; the evil is not the refusal to believe, but the neglect of believing; it is wholly negative; it is exactly what these words describe, "Though He had done so many miracles before them, yet they believed not on Him." These were not the men who attributed His miracles to Beelzebub; who hated His words; who feared that all men would believe on Him. They simply did not believe on Him. They were not the remnant which "took the servants of the king, and used them spitefully, and slew them[a]." Yet they made light of the message, and went their way,

. [a] Matt. xxii. 6.

one to his farm, another to his merchandise. And this leads us to see the modes in which the evil manifests its presence. It may be by leading to a neglect of the revelation as a whole. This was very much the attitude of the Greek or Roman philosopher in the face of the preaching of the Gospel: he cared for none of these things. Whether or not the already well-peopled area which held his allowed divinities admitted into its copious extent the new claimant, was to him a matter of absolute indifference; it in no way touched his life, or would affect his habits, or stir his affections, or move his convictions. He heard the message of salvation impassively, as the unmeaning utterance of a mere babbler; as the unpractical dream of a setter forth of strange gods, whose existence he was ready to admit, because its denial involved a more positive, and so a more troublesome action than its admission. In such men we may read an entire neglect of God's revelation of Himself. And so to a great degree it was with the Jews. He "came unto His own and His own received Him not;" a deep and thorough worldliness had eaten out the receptive faculty of their souls. His words appealed to nothing in themselves which answered to them. It was but when for the moment they fancied that He might deliver them from the Roman yoke, and set up amongst them an earthly king, that they were ready to follow Him. At other times the fame of His mighty deeds, when it did not excite malignant hatred, woke up but a passing curiosity, and the multitude which had followed Him to the mountain melted away again as easily and as unimpressed as it had gathered round Him. And but little different from this is the position of too many

in every Christian country. They have grown up with
the sights and sounds of Christianity around them;
they learned its Creed in their childhood; they have
inherited, in some degree at least, its standard of morals;
and this is all; they deny nothing, and they believe
nothing. In no true sense do they believe in *Him* who
works these miracles before their eyes. It would make
no material difference in their lives if He was not, and if
His faith were not. For the scheme of their lives is con-
structed, and its daily course proceeds, without any refer-
ence to Him; they have no sense of need which He
must satisfy; no feeling of the guilt of sin from which
He must deliver them; no strife with evil for which
He must strengthen them; no aspirations after the fu-
ture, for the fulfilment of which their souls hang on Him;
no secret communion with Him which is dearer to them
than all beside Him. They have taken for granted that
the religion in which they have been brought up is true;
they know that all persons of respectability conform in a
certain way to the standard which it has helped to fix;
they believe it to be useful in maintaining order, in
civilizing the masses, in keeping the poor from discontent
and violence. As an institution they think it is to be
supported. They have no idea of its troubling them;
they have grafted on it their own selfish allowances, and
they are well content, and they think no more about its
message. Here, then, is one plain manifestation of this
neglect of God's revelation. In the real meaning of the
words it is true of such, that " God is not in all their
thoughts."

But there are other manifestations of the same habit.

Thus, for example, there are those to whom the truths
of the Christian faith are by no means these mere un-
controverted unrealities; who have, or at least have had,
convictions more or less distinct and strong of its truth,
but between whom and it there exists a moral contra-
diction; who appreciate its purity, but cannot bring
themselves to abandon impurity; who see that it re-
quires humility and meekness and charity, and who
cannot bring themselves to purge their souls of pride
and self-assertion and wrathfulness; who perceive that
it demands the surrender of their whole heart, and who,
with more or less of consciousness, withhold that surrender, and so who by degrees close their eyes to its
truths, and shut its light out of their souls. Here, then,
is another as real and yet widely divergent manifestation of neglect.

But, once more, there is another and a still more
subtle manifestation of the same evil; when not only is
the general truth of Christianity admitted, but when the
beauty of its morality is perceived, when even its spiri-
tuality is appreciated, but when its distinctive doctrines
are held to be of little moment, so that its spirit is, as
it is thought, retained. Now if the teaching of our
blessed Lord professed to be only an improved code of
morals, or if it merely appealed to the internal spiritual
consciousness of each one who received it, there would
be no neglect of the revelation in such a mode of treatment. But the very reverse of this is the fact. The
distinctive doctrines of our faith are the central part
of the whole revelation, from which emanate all its moral
and spiritual effects. It is pre-eminently a Theology,

a declaration by God concerning Himself. The mystery of the Trinity; the being and relations of the Father, of the Son, and of the Holy Ghost; and flowing from these, the eternal counsels of redemption, the marvel of the atonement, and the grace of sanctification;—these are the mighty truths which flow out into all the various motives which are to act with constraining power upon the renewed heart; and to seek therefore to obtain these without receiving and holding fast that central revelation, is but another manifestation of a subtle but most real neglect of the whole truth.

Here, then, are some of the most prominent forms in which the evil temper which is condemned by the Evangelist is manifested amongst ourselves. I will not stop to try to estimate their prevalence amongst us. Rather would I ask you to look around, and above all within yourselves, and answer for yourselves the question, Do they not abound? Are there not every where these impassive spectators of the mighty miracles of heart and spirit which are wrought daily by His power? these neglecters of His words? these careless and indifferent discussers of doctrine? But leaving this estimate of the prevalence of the evil, let us go on to see;—

II. What are the causes from which it springs.

Now the master cause is, of course, to be found in the blight which has passed upon our fallen nature. If we were as God made us; if the balance of all our various powers and motives and inclinations were held true and even; if the lower parts of our nature, instead of intruding impetuously through appetite and passion upon the higher, were held down in their proper sphere;

and if our spiritual nature were so purified from corruption that it could comprehend and desire its own greatest good, our sense of the blessedness of communion with God would be so strong, that to reject His revelations would be as unnatural to us as it is to the living eye to shun the light. The temptation to such a rejection springs from the disturbance of our own nature; to the drawing down from its true level of our spiritual faculty. Things present, felt, seen, handled, which address themselves to the appetites of the body, which promise to give immediate satisfaction to the lower impulses of the soul, these have so vast an influence with us, their voice is so loud, their instances so urgent, their promises so high, that they cloud over all sight of our true blessedness, or even where some gleams of this break in upon us, they overpower our irresolute will, and seize the mastery of the whole man. In this disturbed state of the affections, it is with the soul as with the body in extreme sickness. The most real things melt into unreality, and the merest phantoms grow into the most absolute realities. This, then, being our state, whatever strengthens the power of the lower faculties of our nature becomes to us a cause of rejecting God's truth. Thus whatever increases in us the love of this present world tends directly to make us neglect God's manifestation of Himself. This is what our Lord teaches the Jews when He says, "How can ye believe, which receive honour one of another, and seek not the honour that cometh of God alone [b]?" And the process is laid bare in the thirty-third and thirty-fourth verses

[b] John v. 44.

of the twelfth chapter of St. John, for there we read that
there were many of the chief rulers who believed on
Him; who saw, that is, that He was the true light,
who were drawn towards that light, and who might have
been led on by it to salvation; but they resisted these
drawings, they stifled these first motions of the Spirit
of grace within themselves, "they did not confess Him,
lest they should be put out of the synagogue: for they
loved the praise of men more than the praise of God[c]."
There was a direct strife in their souls between these
two attractions, and that of the earth was the stronger;
and the effect of this was, that "they could not believe, because their eyes were blinded and their heart
hardened[d]." What a wonderful sight it is, brethren,
which the Gospel narrative thus opens to us! The very
Son of God, the Light of the world, the Father's Word,
the Father's Wisdom, standing amongst men; working
works such as none other had wrought; speaking gra-
cious words which in spite of themselves forced the
hearers to wonder at them; teaching with authority;
declaring by every act His purity and love and power;
and all this no more perceived than are the various
colours of the sunlit day by those who are born blind.
And this darkness, observe further, was upon men who
had in their hands the law and the prophets, and who
gave, as the Pharisees did, their whole lives to the mi-
nute and diligent observance of their every letter. How
fearful an example is this of the way in which the love
of this present world causes a general neglect of God's
revelation of Himself. Thus, whatever binds us to this

[c] John xii. 42, 43.   [d] Ibid. 39, 40.

world is a cause of this darkness. Great occupation, even about lawful and necessary objects, if it is not continually purified by being offered up to God as its truest end, thus shuts out the light. So do, even more, idleness and frivolity, which make the abundance of trifles great and engrossing to our enfeebled minds. Energy and determination of character, therefore, on the one side, devoting themselves to worldly business for itself, do this; levity and indolence, on the other side, do it still more fatally. Pre-eminently is this the case where all the truths of God's revelation have been always known as assumed and uncontradicted propositions; and where, therefore, there can be nothing new, startling, or necessarily awakening about them. For that on which the energies of our minds are expended becomes, through that very action, real to them; whilst that which is, as it were, set aside from that action, grows from its very stillness into a statue-like unreality.

And if this worldliness of our nature thus tends to cause in all of us a general neglect of God's truth, still more is this neglect engendered when its tone contradicts our daily life. It is thus that men come to that second manifestation of which I spoke, when they admit as an intellectual proposition the truth of revelation, but disregard its moral teaching. Every allowed immorality either of the flesh or of the spirit acts back again upon our moral nature, and blunts in us the capacity of discerning right from wrong, and so tends to produce this result. For thus the moral touch becomes obtuse. This is a most grievous curse of sin: its poison ever inflicts upon the soul a moral and spiritual paralysis, until it loses all powers of moral sensation, and so men come to live in sin of every kind; in selfish indolence, in waste of time, in the indulgence of anger, contempt, hatred, or uncleanness, and yet think that they are believers in Christianity. They come, at least at times, to church, hear the Bible read, go through the form of saying prayers, nay, are even, like the old Pharisee who devoured widows' houses, zealous for certain modes of religious observance, and yet live habitually in the absolute neglect of the moral code of Christ's Gospel.

Near akin, again, to this is the cause of that other manifestation of neglect to which I drew your attention, when men make light of the distinctive doctrines of the faith. For just as the moral trial of the last class is concerned mainly with the usurping struggles of the body to assume the supreme government of the man, so in those exposed to this temptation is the main strength of that moral trial in the struggle of the mere intellectual faculty to domineer over the soul. With such men God's revelation is little else than a matter for the exercise of their own intellectual faculties. The form in which it has pleased God to give it to them in the volume of inspiration and in the creeds of the Church makes such a mode of treatment the easier and the more attractive. To the absolute truth revealed they believe that they are ready to bow implicitly, if only they can find out for themselves what that truth is; and so they think themselves at liberty to subject the vehicle in which it is communicated to them to a freedom of scrutiny which continually interferes with either the authority or the meaning of the revelation. This scrutiny gives ample room for the indulgence of the pride of intellect. To this they yield, and as they yield to it it triumphs over them, and soon domineers over the higher faculties of the soul; over its gift of intuition, its powers of loving, of adoring, of worshipping; and as in these chiefly are lodged the power of receiving divine truth, the clear eye of such souls is soon filmed over, they mistake the shadows which soon flit in rainbow lights before them for the real objects on which the gaze should be fixed. All becomes uncertain to them. Doctrine in its clearness passes away as a delusion which once befooled them, and they rest in the persuasion, first, that the value of God's revelation of Himself consists in the impression made upon themselves; and next, that this impression depends more upon their own perceptive faculty than upon the clearness of the outline of the object presented to their view: and thus seeming to themselves still to hold to revelation, they dissolve its outline into their own internal apprehensions of what it ought to be, and so they, too, come in their own way to neglect the revelation of the eternal Son, by substituting for it their own imaginations; and though He hath done so many miracles before them, yet they believe not in Him.

Here, then, are some of the causes which lead to this neglect. Who can doubt that all of them are actively at work amongst us? Surely in a degree which perhaps was never before equalled in the history of mankind, worldliness in its most intense activity is around us, and so must threaten our souls. For on every side it assails us. In the great excitement which politics, science, literature, and society now offer to every one of us; in the physical

enjoyments which wealth, civilization, and abundance
bring so close to us; there are undoubtedly ever present
with us the actively employed instruments of a most
intense form of worldliness.

If, then, this first cause of the neglect of revelation
is with us, the others I have traced out with you are not
wanting. There is, I think, we cannot doubt, a very
common and very prevalent standard of morality widely
different from that of Christ's Gospel. Cast but your
eyes around you where you will, and say if this is not so.
Do not our often lamented and yet almost unmitigated
social evils discredit Christendom? Or if you will look
closer to yourselves, are not the indolence, and the pro-
fusion, and the self-indulgence which is so common in
our own society, most unlike the tempers of Gethsemane
and the bitter Mount of Calvary? And again, is there
not within our own borders a freedom of religious specu-
lation which scarcely leaves untransmuted so much as
one article of the Creed of the apostles?

But, III. let us note the consequences of this evil. For
where its causes are so actively at work, must it not be
the bounden duty of the watchman on our walls to sound
the note of warning and strive to awaken a sense of the
real effects of an evil so likely to spread on all sides
its unsuspected presence?

For it is no little evil. It is indeed the loss of all.
In whatever form it is manifested, the neglect of God's
revelation by those to whom He has offered it is the rejection of Christ, and that is the rejection of salvation.
It is this which we so greatly need to see. That common life which does really put Christianity aside; which

steals on so quietly with its even flow ; but into which the
faith of Christ never enters as a constraining motive ;
which knows no earnestness in prayer, no deep con-
trition, no struggle with sin, no grasp of faith upon the
cross, it is not the life of a true servant of Christ. It is
in truth, however we may try to disguise it from ourselves, the life of one who, though all the miracles of
Christ are wrought before his eyes, does not believe in
Him. And surely this is the greatest indignity which
we can put on Him. For if God has given to us a
revelation, He must have given it in His love for the
receiver. It must be as much meant by God for him
as the natural light is meant for the enlightenment of
his natural eye ; and for him therefore to neglect it, is to
do the highest conceivable dishonour to its giver. Thus
there is indeed a contempt of God in that which at first
sight seems to be so little marked with the more malignant features of sin as does this passing by of revelation.
Moreover, besides its present contempt of God, there is
in such a life a wilful casting away of what is essential
to the fitting our own characters for the presence of
God hereafter. For the Gospel revelation is that which
God's love has given for this purpose. It is " the power
of God unto salvation." It is what His wisdom has
provided as the means of our restoration to His image :
and in letting that pass by us unused, we let slip the
opportunity of restoration. This was our Master's
warning to the Jews : " Yet a little while is the light
with you. Walk while ye have the light, lest darkness
come upon you °." And that darkness does come. Not

° John xii. 35.

only is the light itself removed, but there is a peculiar darkening of the eye in those who have the light and do not use it. It is with the souls of such men as it is with the bodies of certain lower animals, which have withdrawn themselves into rayless caverns afar from the light of day: they were plainly formed by their Creator's hand to see, but their long absence from the light has obliterated the power of vision, so that at times even the very visual organs themselves become extinct. And so is it with these souls. Neglect of the revelation even in the lower stages of such carelessness leads on, by small and unmarked but inevitable steps, to contempt of it altogether. The gradations are well-nigh imperceptible, but the end is sure.

And as this is true of a general neglect, so is it true of negligence as to the moral precepts of the revelation. Men soon acquire a frightful power of combining correct views, and even occasional feelings, with a most debased standard of action as to their own besetting sins, whatever they are, if they allow themselves once to set out on this evil path. Every religious advantage becomes to such an one but an instrument of his degradation. His acquaintance with Holy Scripture, his chapel prayers, his occasional Communions, if they are combined with a giving way to his own temptations, be they to sloth, or sensuality, or ill-temper, or mere frivolous living, tend to harden the heart and to deaden the conscience. Oh, how many, even before they are launched hence into the open sea of life, have already fixed their character into a settled neglect of the message of salvation. The woe of Chorazin and of Bethsaida is upon such hearts.

It must be indeed a miracle of God's mercy which alone can arouse them from this fatal negligence.

Nor is the consequence of the last neglect to which I have drawn your notice really less destructive. It is not difficult to trace the course of such a man. As the gratification of the pride of intellect was a main part of man's original temptation, and a principal instrument in effecting his fall, so is the abasing of that pride a main instrument of his restoration. He cannot be really great till he knows his littleness; for he cannot be great except in communion with God, Who only is great, and he cannot hold that communion with God while he seeks to be as God—knowing for himself, and by his own choosing, good and evil. Christ's Gospel, therefore, is to every man who receives it truly a humbling, and because a humbling, an exalting revelation. The man that would receive it must know that he is poor, and blind, and naked. He must come, as guilty, for pardon, as defiled, for cleansing. This, and this only, is indeed to come to Christ,—to believe in Him; for believing in Him is to believe in Him as He is, not as our fancy would paint Him to be. If we believe not in Him as suffering for the guilty, as offering Himself for us, as by His death and passion, and sufferings and wounds, working out our salvation, we believe not in Him, but in some shadowy substitute of our own imagination, to whom, instead of to Himself, we pay our homage.

Here, then, is the deadly consequence of yielding in matters of faith to the pride of intellect. Gorgeous often is the vision which rises up before the imagination of such idol-worshippers. Fixing the whole gaze of their soul indeed upon themselves, they thrust that self, which they have invested with all heavenly splendours, between themselves and the Cross of the Crucified. They believe themselves to be rising daily to higher measures of spiritual illumination; they dream of direct communings, without the intervention of any Mediator, with the unapproachable God; they deem the simple faith which cheers the soul of the believer to be an infantine state of spiritual existence which they have left long behind them. The blood of sprinkling, the Cross of Calvary, the pierced hands, the wounded side,—these have vanished from their eyes; they may suit inferior minds, incapable of supporting the clear atmosphere and unimpeded vision into which they think themselves to have entered. And yet what is all this but to have lost sight of Him in the sight of Whom alone is salvation? What is it but to have reached the old height of Sadducean sanctity, and to sit down with them who, "though He had done so many miracles before them, yet believed not on Him?"

If, then, these are our dangers, I. in themselves, II. in their causes, and III. in their consequence, where, IV. shall we find our safeguard?

The first great safety is in the sight of the danger: in perceiving that, not in hearing about religion, not in talking about it, not in belonging to this party or to that, but in being indeed Christ's believing and obedient servants ourselves, is any safety: in understanding and remembering that the faith of Christ, if it is to save us, must be to us not merely an external tradition, but a reproduction in ourselves by the very power of God the Holy Ghost, in our hearts and consciences, and spirit and life. And then, beyond this, the guards which under God will save us from a deadly neglect, are the common instruments of the spiritual life in the renewed soul. They are matters so obvious that they must sound trite as I name them, and yet it is of God's great love that it is through such common things, which are within the reach of all, that we are saved. They are watchfulness against temptation; against the power of sense and appetite; against the benumbing presence of indolence in such ordinary things as attendance at the chapel or the lecture room where for the time our lot is cast. Through the discipline of such common acts this deadly disorder of neglect may, not all at once, but by degrees, be cured. Only our watchfulness against these evils, and our endeavours to do these right things, must be based not on mere expediency or a regard to the propriety of our own characters, but from a desire to please God; that is, on a principle of faith, however weak as yet the faith may be in us: they must be done as acts which we offer up to our blessed Saviour, and then, through His grace, every one of them will be to us an assistance against the danger of neglecting God's manifestation of Himself. And to obtain this gift of living faith we must ask it of God in prayer: in prayer made real by being breathed out of the heart with earnestness of desire, and being united, at least in the endeavour of a conscious act, with the intercession of our Lord. There must be, too, the lifting up the soul to God the Holy Ghost that He may breathe over it His renewing influences. All things will help one who is thus simply striving in the use of common things to do God's will. His daily business will become full of God; his successes will be occasions for hearty praise; above all, times of sorrow, depression, and disappointment will become special opportunities for winning some more real sense of things unseen. Through them God will cleanse for us the atmosphere around us from its ordinary worldly heaviness, in order to make manifest to us the sunlit towers of the heavenly Jerusalem. For He does work with and for those who will thus work for themselves. But above all, there must be in every man who would overcome this neglect earnest self-denial. He must force himself to give up something for God. In instances beyond number, it is indeed listlessness which leads to neglect, as neglect leads to destruction. And what we need to gain is earnestness of present purpose, and earnestness of present purpose God gives to us through His blessing on this discipline of self-denial.

Without this we cannot overcome the desperate worldliness of our nature. Most men wish, in a sort of idle dreamy way, to be some time or other better; to be leading a more real life. They would not be content to appear before the judgment-seat as they are; perhaps they pray to be delivered from the rule of this present world : but they do not mean to be delivered *now*, and to be delivered altogether. If God made them the offer they would not accept it. They would ask to have a little more licence for indulgence first; to follow Christ, but not just yet; to follow Him after going back to see first those of their household, the familiar pleasures and indulgences of their worldly life. This, through God's grace, must be overcome: and one vigorous, hearty course of earnest prayer, and present self-denial, would overcome it, and would save us. For as we fought against this dream of worldliness, God would fight for us. He would shew us His love, and that would kindle ours, and under its fire all other hindrances would be burnt up as the thorns in the furnace flame. For love is THE guard against neglect; love reads all mysteries plain; to love, all labours are easy; with love, neglect cannot co-exist. "For love is of God, and every one that loveth is born of God, and knoweth God."

SERMON II.

Doubts as to the Revelation.

ST. JOHN xx. 27.

"AND BE NOT FAITHLESS, BUT BELIEVING."

I LED your thoughts last Sunday to one special trial
which must beset those to whom God vouchsafes
a revelation of His Nature and His Will; the temptation, I mean, from various causes and in various ways, to
neglect the gift. I wish this morning to consider with
you a kindred subject; another temptation to which the
receiver of revelation must be exposed,—the temptation
to doubts about religion. And first let me beg you
to observe that such doubts are very various in their
origin and in their character.

There are the doubts which are the fruit of an evil
life, which come forth as the obscene creatures of the
night come forth—because it is the night; because the
darkness is abroad, and they are the creatures of the
darkness. These are, for the most part, self-chosen
doubts, bred of corruption and of fear; of a clinging to
sin and yet of a fear of its punishment; of a conscious
resistance to the ways and works of a God of purity
and truth; of an evil interest in finding revelation to
be false, because it is a system which if true is fatally
opposed to them. Men pursued by these doubts are
a fearful spectacle. The terrors which at times shake

them are often appalling to witness; and yet even these
are less awful than the forced grimace with which they
try to laugh them off. Vaunting their doubts, like the
lonely wanderer who sings noisily to conceal or overcome his fear of the darkness, that they may, if possible, scatter by the loudness of their laugh the besetting
crowd of their alarms.

Here, then, are one set of doubts. But it is not of
these that I would speak further to-day. Nor would
I dwell to-day on a second class, which, however, I must
mention, in order to clear the way for my proper subject. There are, then, doubts as to religious truth
which are in many respects the direct opposites of those
of which I have just spoken; which, instead of being
the resource of evil, are the trouble of holy souls; which
whether the result of a peculiar constitution of body or
of mind, or the fruit of an unhappy training, or the
bitter consequence of past sin, rise unbidden, like the
black motes which in the gladdest sunshine will trouble
a disordered vision, even in the clearest daylight of faith
or the warmest glow of devotion; which are striven
with, prayed against, and at last overcome, as the bright-
ening intuition of faith is gradually purged of such
interrupting specks. Souls thus afflicted need the ten-
derest care, and the wisest and most loving discipline.
But it is not of them that I would speak further to-day.

It is against doubts of yet another character that,
God helping me, I would now warn you. And this
I would do, because I believe that their presence, and
even their indulgence, is at this moment by no means
rare amongst us; because their true character is often

disguised under the most specious forms; because they thus seize upon the unwary; because the young, and amongst the young, the generous, the ardent, the thoughtful, and the enquiring, are often their special victims; and because their course is one of weakness, both intellectual and spiritual, whilst their end, where they triumph, is misery here, and too often everlasting loss hereafter. Oh! that on any tempted to such doubts who may hear me now, especially if as yet they are but entering on the evil way, the God of hope may bestow through my words some measure of His great gift of calm, unquestioning, believing peace.

The doubts, then, of which I speak are those which address themselves to specific and clearly revealed points in the revelation which yet as a whole the doubting man does not disbelieve. There is always place for such doubts. For overwhelming as is the evidence for the Christian revelation as a whole, there is as to many particular parts of it, even where its declarations are most explicit, room for question and for cavil. This will be no matter of wonder to those who remember how large a part of the probation of every man consists in the trial of his faith, and of all those moral habits of meekness, truth, simplicity, teachableness, and the like, which faith produces. It is, then, consistent with our reason that there should be such difficulties, and that they do exist is indisputable. For, first, many of the truths which God has revealed are strange to our fallen nature; and, next, it has pleased Him that the divine revelation should everywhere be mingled in its delivery with a human element. Wherever our uninstructed reason rebels against the message there must be a temptation to, and where-ever the human element intervenes, there must be opportunity for, question. Thus, for example, God's Word is spoken to us and recorded for us through the intervention of human agents. It is recorded in human manuscripts; it is read by us out of a printed book. Here at every turn is opportunity for doubt and question. So, too, the great doctrines of the faith are recorded for us in Creeds and Confessions drawn up by men. They grew up gradually. They were drawn forth from the implicit faith of the Church unwillingly, at uncertain intervals, often after grievous strife and disputing. There are varieties in their tone and expressions. Upon many, and those often the deepest points, there is manifestly, as time passes on, an increasing definiteness of language, which was attained under the assaults of heretics on the truth and its defence by the faithful. From this peculiar process the history of what is really the fixing of the Church's terminology in matters of belief often appears at first sight to be the fixing of its faith. Here, again, at every turn there is room for question and doubt.

Nay, more; it may often seem that these doubts are but the pauses of modesty, and these questions the interrogations of an enquiring faith. Thus the doubts are cherished and encouraged under the garb of piety; until a habit is formed in the mind of subjecting the written Word and the authoritative declarations of the faith to the scrutiny of each man's intellectual faculties, and, according to their decision, to his acceptance, modification, or rejection of them. Now

such a mode of dealing with revelation is exceedingly
attractive. It promises to make the faith so rational;
to give every man so good a reason for the hope that is
in him; to be so free from all forcing of doctrines on
him, that it naturally wins to itself young and ardent
minds. Yet it is against this that I would so earnestly warn you; and that for this reason, I. that in its
very first principle it is subversive of all true faith, and
that it is therefore in its consequences full of ruin to
the soul.

For observe what is involved in it. It implies that
each man to whom the revelation is proposed has within
himself powers which enable, and so which require, him
to decide whether its separate propositions, however
distinctly they may be stated, are or are not such as
they ought to be. It makes him the judge of the
fitness of the statement, not the receiver of the statement as true because it is the word of its giver. It
makes the single receptive eye, without regard to its
health or its disease, the judge of the existence of
colour. Thus in principle it destroys all authority in
the revelation; and so whilst it professes to admit
the revelation as a whole, it dissolves in one universal
mist of doubtfulness all the definiteness of its particular
teaching. Thus to treat revelation is in truth to lose
sight of its essential character, and to deal with it as
a philosophy; that is to say, as a theory which is to be
received, refuted, or modified according to the receiver's
apprehension of its intrinsic reasonableness. For this
is what the framer of a philosophy must do; what more
or less every one who is even following up the philo-

sophical speculations of others must do. He has to read
off into a theory the language of facts from observed
phenomena. To a great extent the confirmations of
a long experience give a sort of certainty to a theory
so obtained; and yet at any moment a new fact may
require its modification or abandonment. But revelation
is concerned with matters beyond our observation, and
must be received, if received at all, on the authority of
the giver. The province of the intellect with regard to
it is, first, to examine its authority, and then to comprehend, so far as they admit of comprehension, its several
propositions. To go one step beyond this, and to en-
courage the intellectual faculty to intrude into the do-
main of authority with its doubts as to the fitness of
any part of the message, is really to uproot the whole
foundation on which alone revelation can rest. Most
striking are the words in which the capacious intellect
and strong faith of St. Augustine stated of old this truth.
Contrasting the certainty of revelation with the uncertainty of the philosophy of the new Academics, " Qui-
bus," he says, " incerta sunt omnia ;" he continues,
" Omnino Civitas Dei talem dubitationem tamquam de-
mentiam detestatur." And then, having shewn that
a reasonable trust in the evidence of the senses was
at the foundation of all belief, he describes in these few
grand words the Christian man's certainty : " Credit
etiam Scripturis Sanctis et Veteribus et Novis, quas
canonicas appellamus, unde fides ipsa concepta est, ex
qua justus vivit; per quam sine dubitatione ambulamus
quamdiu peregrinamur a Domino ᵃ."

ᵃ De Civitate Dei, lib. xix. cap. 18.

Very little reflection, I think, may convince any one
how evidently this law is stamped on every part of the
Christian revelation. For it teaches nothing merely to
gratify our curiosity. In this respect it is the exact
opposite of nature. For the handwriting of the Creator,
in His works of nature, seems to be imprinted on them
for the very purpose of stimulating our curiosity, and
training and rewarding our powers of investigation and
discovery. In the Christian revelation, on the other
hand, nothing is revealed for the sake merely of its being
known, but that the degree of knowledge given us may
in some way or other affect our moral and spiritual
training. Every page of the Bible opens questions to
which it gives no solution; it tells us, for instance,
what sin is in its essence and in its evil, in order that
we may learn to hate and resist it, but it never tells us
how it comes to exist in the world of a God at once
Almighty and All-good. Teaching all the highest results
of the highest philosophy, Holy Scripture passes pur-
posely by all the questions with starting and dis-
cussing which philosophy delights to entangle its fol-
lowers in the net of curious enquiry. Pre-eminently
may we notice this in the treatment of all such matters
by Him who was the Light of light, the living Word
of the everlasting Father. They often met Him in the
questions of the curious, and they received always
answers of the same tone :—" Whose wife shall she be
of the seven?" led but to the rebuke, "Ye do err, not
knowing the Scriptures, nor the power of God. For
in the resurrection they neither marry nor are given
in marriage, but are as the angels of God in heaven [b]."

[b] Matt. xxii. 28—30.

How sublime is the tone of spiritual rebuke and instruction here, which, whilst it puts down the prying curiosity of the carping doubter, lifts up the whole argument into a higher region of thought and feeling. So was it always. When " One said unto Him,"—for the satisfaction, as it seems, of a mere curiosity,—"Lord, are there few that be saved? He said unto them,"—turning the empty craving for information into an earnest exhortation to a higher practice,—"Strive to enter in at the strait gate; for many"—with a direct glance at these speculative dreamers—" will seek to enter in, and shall not be able[c]." And at times the tones are sterner yet. "Lord, what shall this man do? What is that to thee, follow thou Me[d]." Or take the question of the whole faithful eleven, "Lord, wilt thou at this time restore again the kingdom to Israel?" and see how it is answered,— "It is not for you to know the times or the seasons, which the Father hath put in His own power[e]."

Always this is the tone. It seems to say, as His own Apostle learned afterwards to write, "But foolish questions avoid[f]." Or, as it was summed up by the man of God of old, " Secret things belong unto the Lord our God: but those things which are revealed belong unto us and to our children for ever, *that we may do all the words of this law*[g]." And all this involves the great principle that revelation gives us an insight into the mighty truths of the spiritual world for the sake of training the heart, not of gratifying the intellect. It suggests to us that the mysteries as to which it gives us the hints needful for our practice are too vast to be fully comprehended by

[c] Luke xiii. 23.   [d] John xxi. 21, 22.
[e] Acts i. 6.   [f] 2 Tim. ii. 23.   [g] Deut. xxix. 29.

us here, and that our business is to receive those hints humbly, believing that what they teach when we receive them the most literally, must be the nearest approach to the truth which we are here capable of making, and that to endeavour to extract from them more than this simple teaching by the processes of the intellect, is to misconceive both of it and of them. It is to misconceive of them, because, as we have seen, they are given for another end ; and of it, because the mere intellect cannot deal profitably with them, for the natural man receiveth not the things of the Spirit, neither can he know them, because they are spiritually discerned ; and he who so uses his mere intellect is like the workman who employs his tools on matter for which they were not framed, and who therefore mars his work and blunts his instruments. The intellect, for its own perfection, needs the discipline and certainty of dealing steadily with facts and honestly with authority, and it therefore is injured, as well as its result falsified, when it is encouraged to speculate where it ought to observe, and to question where it ought to receive.

Here, then, is the first great caution against allowing anywhere this habit of doubtfulness. It involves a principle which is destructive of all true faith, and so is utterly at variance with the very idea of revelation, and especially with the tone of that which God has given to us.

But II. To allow these doubts is no barren admission of a faulty principle. From the very nature of the case, the habit of doubting, when once it has been formed, must grow and increase. For the mind which has once been put into this attitude of suspicious observation, must find in the marvel of revelation ever new subjects for question. It is but the smallest part of the mysteries of the eternal world which can be grasped by our feeble faculties. On every side of that which we can reach is that which is inaccessible; all around the single point we see is evermore sweeping by us and surging in the darkness the unresting, immeasureable ocean-tide of the hidden counsels of the incomprehensible Lord. Once let the mind, instead of receiving humbly, begin to doubt, and doubt will be everywhere. The struggles of such a soul in the uncertainty around it are like the plunging of the maddened herd into the boundless morass. Every effort engulphs in the quagmire more of the surrounding sward, and sinks the powerless victims in ruin. Doubt once yielded to perpetually increases for itself the area over which it acts, multiplies the subjects on which it seizes, and weakens the power of resistance in the soul. In the course of this process even the intellectual powers suffer grievous injury. For, by degrees, doubt eats out the very power of weighing evidence, and a baffling sense of universal uncertainty, like the oppressive presence of a fog, benumbs the acting of the intellect.

The very testimony of his senses becomes suspicious to such a man, and then the world around him grows into an entangled enigma. Nay, he may come to doubt even of his own existence. The keenest intellectual powers lose their edge in such an atmosphere; no tempers are more widely apart than that of the philosopher who is building up and establishing truths by patient enquiry and a perpetual solving of mysteries, and that of the questioning sceptic, who is unsettling all that he touches.

But more. Whilst it is thus injurious to the intellect, the indulgence of doubts leads to a moral ruin to which there is no limit. The man who is possessed by such a spirit comes in time to doubt whether there be a right or a wrong in anything. The poison spreads even to his affections, and to all the relations of life around which the living tendrils of those affections ought to be instinctively entwined. He comes to question the reality of love between parent and child, between husband and wife. For trace up any affection far enough, and it leads, in the mystery of our being, to some strange connection with ourselves, and may thus be resolved into the subtlest essence of a very sordid selfishness, and so lose its generous nature, and even its moral truth. And to this destructive analysis of all his purer and higher feelings the doubter may be driven on until he can believe in no affection, and only see, under the rosy hues of the purest earthly love, the hideous spectacle of humanity resolving itself into the hateful grossness of the meanest sensuality and the merest animal excitement. Such a moral sickness I have more than once been called upon to heal. And most difficult it is to treat. For such a man has dug with his speculations into the ground into which the affections of his heart sink their roots of mystery, until he has destroyed their vitality. And how in one thus morally debased can any spiritual life continue? All the facts of the spiritual world around him, from which his own spiritual life was to draw its sustenance, have melted into shadows. Instead of the Almighty Father's love, the Eternal Son's atonement, and the Blessed Spirit's presence and work, instead of all around him beaming, and kindling, and flashing with the manifested love of a revealed and covenant God, there is the dreamy notion of a possible absorption into a possible pervading essence; and with this loss of the definiteness of the articles of the Christian Creed, all its power evaporates. The mist which thus gathers round the great truth of God dissolves its clear brilliancy into a mere vapoury cloud, until it has no longer shape, or light, or warmth, wherewith to cheer, illuminate, and animate creation.

Oh! believe me, brethren, the havoc wrought in this soul for which Christ died is indeed awful. Set him for yourself in thought beside the humblest believer in Christ, and see what he has lost. Surely to understand this it were enough to place the calm, childlike peacefulness of the most untaught believer beside the heart-eating, questioning uncertainty of the other at any moment of his existence. But do more than this, that you may see yet more plainly all the loss. Look at these two in the hour of some great trouble, which is really trying the foundation of their being. Think of them when earthly sorrow has come very nigh to them, and laid upon them its heaviest burdens; when the grave is yet open in which have just been laid all that made life dear to them: think of them when the sharp arrow of conviction of sin has just struck its barbed point into the soul; when they wander about hither and thither heart-stricken, seeking rest and finding none: put them both in your thought into such terrors as these, and what has the doubter to turn to then? Listen to his attempt to pray, and hear his quivering lips stammer forth the doubter's prayer—"O God, if indeed there be a God, help me in my misery, if indeed there be any such being as I deem myself to be." Place beside such an utterance of a fully developed uncertainty the cry of the child's heart, as, coming with boldness through the blood of Jesus, it reaches forth to its heavenly Father, not doubting of the presence, the love, the tenderness, the care, the knowledge, and the power of the reconciled God and Father to whom it breathes forth its sob of sorrow,—and see if the loss of the doubter is not great indeed.

But go one step further, and see, if you would know the uttermost extremity of his loss, what is the doubter's death. It is always awful to meet great and unchangeable realities with which we have trifled as if they were meaningless shadows. And what a meeting with them is there upon that deathbed, when conscience, at last awake, is crowding on the astonished memory the record of a life's transgressions; when the enemy is accusing and tormenting the soul, which is all but his own; when the terrible summons to the judgment of the just God, like the low deep voices of advancing thunder-clouds, is beginning to shake the heart; when to have a firm hold on one sure promise; when to cling to the hem of the Healer's garment; when to see, as the ransom of a multitude of sins, the blood of His wounded side, would be indeed the soul's only and its sufficient refuge: then in that hour of agony to be compassed about with self-chosen doubts; to have the refinements, and the subtleties, and the questions, and the uncertainties which the man had taken to himself instead of God's sure word of promise and of the atoning blood, gather in troops around him like the very fiends of the pit snatching for his soul; to have some doubt ever intervening between his eager grasp and every promise, between his wretched soul and every vision of the Lord Jesus Christ; to have all this and to find no escape from it; to have lost the power of believing, and to know, when it is too late to win it, that it is lost for ever; to have in that hour, at best, " thy life hang in doubt before thee [h]," because only that sure definiteness of a fixed faith which thou hast thrown away can shelter thee in that shock; to have, too probably, thy doubts close in upon thee in an unutterable despair, —this is to die the doubter's death. From such a death may the good Lord of His great mercy deliver us.

It is from this, brethren, that I would help to save you. It is with this you are unawares trifling, when you open your soul to the first plausible approaches of the habit of doubting; it is this harvest of despair for which they are sowing who fling broad-cast into the open furrows of young and generous natures the deadly seeds of doubtfulness. Oh, cruel and most fatal labour! For by no after act of his can the teacher root out of the heart of another the seed of death which he has planted in it. Surely for such above others was the caution written, " Whoso shall make to stumble one of these little ones, it were better for him that a millstone were hanged about his neck, and that he were drowned in the depth of the sea [i]."

[h] Deut. xxviii. 66.　　　　　　[i] Matt. xxviii. 6.

It is not from the imagination that I have drawn this warning. I can tell you of an overshadowed grave which closed in on such a struggle and such an end as that at which I have glanced. In it was laid a form which had hardly reached the fulness of earliest manhood. That young man had gone young, ardent, and simply faithful to the tutelage of one, himself I doubt not a sincere believer, but who sought to reconcile the teaching of our Church, in which he ministered, with the dreams of rationalism. His favourite pupil learned his lore, and it sufficed for his needs whilst health beat high in his youthful veins. But on him sickness and decay closed early in, and, as the glow of health faded, the intellectual lights for which he had exchanged the simplicity of faith began to pale; whilst the viper brood of doubts which almost unawares he had let slip into his soul, crept forth from their hiding-places and raised against him fearfully their envenomed heads. And they were too strong for him. The teacher who had suggested could not remove them; and in darkness and despair his victim died before his eyes the doubter's death.

Of the true mode of resisting and overcoming this fatal evil when it assaults our souls, there is not now, brethren, time for me to speak at any length. If it please God, I may possibly do this hereafter. Only let me now suggest a few of the most prominent safeguards. And, first, this,—that we believe firmly that no one who strives earnestly and aright against doubts as to the faith of Christ need be overcome by them. They are a necessity to no man. And then, secondly, let me say, if he would overcome he must be in earnest in his strife, and not a trifler with it; for the trifler invites temptation, and it

is the earnest-hearted whom God aids, and those whom
He aids not man cannot help. Next, he that would overcome must strive aright. For which, above all, it is
necessary that he should recognise that against which
he strives as a temptation of the Evil One. He must
understand that the mere harbouring, and still more the
yielding, to such doubts is failing in his moral and spiritual probation. This is what our Lord teaches us in
those words of power, "Be not faithless, but believing." For they were spoken to one who was assaulted
by, and who to a certain degree had yielded to such
doubts. From slight indications contained in the
Gospels we may gather that in this questioning habit
lay the chief infirmity of the Apostle St. Thomas.
Circumstances had given it power against him; the
greatness of his love to his Lord, the superabounding
joy which would be his if indeed that Lord were risen
from the dead,—even these strengthened his natural
temptation to question the truth of so marvellous a fact,
which was presented to him on human testimony only.
'How could it be?' asked his unsubdued reason. 'Was
it indeed certain that it had been? might he not make
allowance for the degree in which affection to their
Master's person, longing for His return, the impetuous-
ness of one leading mind, the intense love of another,
the exaggerations and proneness to credulity which he
had noted in others, would so naturally bias their testimony, and justify him in demanding further evidence?'
How do all such plausible suggestions vanish under-
neath the words, "Be not faithless, but believing." The
questioning habit, then, in the eye of Christ is the an-
tagonist of faith. They are set opposite the one to the

other. If you would have one you must mortify the other. Here, then, is the mode of striving rightly against doubt. Treat it as a temptation of the enemy; deal with it as you would with any other of his frauds; watch against it, work against it, pray against it; beware of the company, the books, the teachers, the trains of thought by which you know from past experience that it is encouraged in yourself. See that it is a weakness, not a strength; a blemish, not a beauty; not a glory, but a shame. Beware, then, of it; and above all, for then your strength is greatest, beware of it in its beginnings. And join to your watching the strength of prayer; bring in the power of God to aid you in the strife. Faith in all its degrees and actings is His gift, the work of His Spirit within us; let your prayer be rather, "Lord, increase our faith," than 'Lord, increase our knowledge.'

And since it is "to him that hath" that more " is given," work as well as pray. The first acts of a life of faith, and the last acts of a life of unbelief, are alike within our power. The many disciples who " went back" of old,—because His saying concerning the eating of His flesh and drinking of His blood was hard to their questioning unbelief,—and "walked no more after Him[k]," acted upon no compulsion; but under the leading of their own evil heart of unbelief turned away from Him with whom, if they had remained, He would by His Word, by His presence, by His grace, and by His love, have led them on step by step until He had overcome their doubts, and given them a living faith and the joy of His salvation. But they " went back;" they walked no more after Him; and they perished. And

[k] John vi. 66.

ever so it is with us. He who, when a doubt assails him, yields to it; who, as doubts multiply, intermits his prayers, is less frequent at communion, becomes more conversant with bolder speculations, and allows the growing thought that reason contradicts revelation, is indeed " going back" and " walking no more after" Christ. But he who resists the entrance of doubt, who flings it from him as if it were a loaded shell shot into the fortress of his soul; who in acts of holy obedience, prayer and aspiration, in devout meditation on God's Word, in the frequent utterance of the glowing ascriptions into which the " Gloria Patri et Filio et Spiritui Sancto" turns the dryness of the Creed; who in the Holy Communion of his Master's Body and Blood, seeks indeed to " walk after" his Lord,—he will be kept by Him to salvation. One by one his doubts shall vanish, as the mist of the morning on the mountain's brow, beneath the rising brightness of His revealed presence; in the last struggle and the dying strife He shall be the closest and the most sustaining. Then there shall be a rest in His paradise, where doubts enter not, nor aught which can defile the souls which are safe under His hand; and then the glorious end; the sight of Him as He is; and those words of wonder and of love which shall thrill through the transforming framework of the resurrection body, " Blessed are they who have not seen, and yet have believed."